WHOOPI GOLDBERG

The African-American Biographies series

MAYA ANGELOU
More Than a Poet
0-89490-684-4

LOUIS ARMSTRONG
King of Jazz
0-89490-997-5

ARTHUR ASHE
Breaking the Color
Barrier in Tennis
0-89490-689-5

BENJAMIN BANNEKER
Astronomer and Mathematician
0-7660-1208-5

RALPH BUNCHE
Winner of the
Nobel Peace Prize
0-7660-1203-4

W. E. B. DU BOIS
Champion of Civil Rights
0-7660-1029-3

DUKE ELLINGTON
Giant of Jazz
0-89490-691-7

ARETHA FRANKLIN
Motown Superstar
0-89490-686-0

WHOOPI GOLDBERG
Comedian and Movie Star
0-7660-1205-0

LORRAINE HANSBERRY
Playwright and Voice of Justice
0-89490-945-2

LANGSTON HUGHES
Poet of the
Harlem Renaissance
0-89490-815-4

ZORA NEALE HURSTON
Southern Storyteller
0-89490-685-2

QUINCY JONES
Musician, Composer, Producer
0-89490-814-6

BARBARA JORDAN
Congresswoman, Lawyer,
Educator
0-89490-692-5

MARTIN LUTHER KING, JR.
Leader for
Civil Rights
0-89490-687-9

CORETTA SCOTT KING
Striving for
Civil Rights
0-89490-811-1

TONI MORRISON
Nobel Prize-Winning
Author
0-89490-688-7

WALTER DEAN MYERS
Writer for Real Teens
0-7660-1206-9

JESSE OWENS
Track and Field Legend
0-89490-812-X

COLIN POWELL
Soldier and Patriot
0-89490-810-3

PAUL ROBESON
Actor, Singer,
Political Activist
0-89490-944-4

JACKIE ROBINSON
Baseball's Civil Rights
Legend
0-89490-690-9

IDA B. WELLS-BARNETT
Crusader Against Lynching
0-89490-947-9

OPRAH WINFREY
Talk Show Legend
0-7660-1207-7

CARTER G. WOODSON
Father of African-American History
0-89490-946-0

WHOOPI GOLDBERG

Comedian and Movie Star

Series Consultant:
Dr. Russell L. Adams, Chairman
Department of Afro-American Studies, Howard University

William Caper

Enslow Publishers, Inc.

44 Fadem Road   PO Box 38
Box 699   Aldershot
Springfield, NJ 07081   Hants GU12 6BP
USA   UK
http://www.enslow.com

Publisher's Note

In her autobiographical *Book*, Whoopi Goldberg writes: "I am not an African American. I'm not from Africa. I'm from New York." Out of respect for Whoopi Goldberg, in the pages of this biography the editors will use the term *black*, rather than *African American*.

Copyright © 1999 by William Caper

All rights reserved.

No part of this book may be reproduced by any means without the written permission of the publisher.

Library of Congress Cataloging-in-Publication Data

Caper, William.
    Whoopi Goldberg : comedian and movie star / William Caper.
       p. cm. — (African-American biographies)
    Filmography: p.
    Includes bibliographical references and index.
    Summary: Examines the life and career of the versatile actress and comedian who overcame a drug addiction and became the first black female Academy Award winner since 1939.
    ISBN 0-7660-1205-0
    1. Goldberg, Whoopi, 1955–   —Juvenile literature. 2. Comedians—United States—Biography—Juvenile literature. 3. Afro-American comedians—United States—Biography—Juvenile literature. 4. Motion picture actors and actresses—United States—Biography—Juvenile literature. 5. Afro-American motion picture actors and actresses—United States—Biography—Juvenile literature. [1. Goldberg, Whoopi, 1955–   . 2. Comedians. 3. Actors and actresses. 4. Afro-Americans—Biography. 5. Women—Biography.]   I. Title. II. Series.
PN2287.G578C36 1999
791.43'028'092—dc21
[B]   98-30306
                                         CIP
                                       AC

Printed in the United States of America

10 9 8 7 6 5 4 3 2 1

To Our Readers:

All Internet addresses in this book were active and appropriate when we went to press. Any comments or suggestions can be sent by e-mail to Comments@enslow.com or to the address on the back cover.

Illustration Credits: Cara Metz, pp. 19, 23, 43, 53; Courtesy of Photofest, pp. 9, 14, 31, 36, 61, 64, 70, 77, 83, 87, 91, 100, 104; PLAYBILL® is a registered trademark of Playbill Incorporated, N.Y.C. All rights reserved. Used by permission, pp. 49, 108.

Cover Illustration: Courtesy of Photofest

CONTENTS

1

A Big Night
at the Oscars

t was March 25, 1991, the night the Academy Awards for 1990 were being presented. People everywhere tuned in their televisions to watch some of Hollywood's biggest stars arrive at the Shrine Auditorium in Los Angeles, California. The Academy Award, or Oscar, is the highest honor people in the film business can receive. Tonight's Oscar ceremony was meant to be particularly special because it also celebrated one hundred years of moviemaking.

On the other side of the world the Persian Gulf War was being fought, but a cease-fire had been in effect for a week. Even so, because of the war, security at the

Oscars was high. Each year hundreds of movie fans wait outside the auditorium, sitting on bleachers, hoping to catch a glimpse of the arriving stars. Usually the fans are permitted to take seats the day before the ceremony. But this year no one was allowed onto the bleachers until eight o'clock that morning, and they were not allowed to carry drinks, food, binoculars, or even cameras. In addition, everyone entering the auditorium—no matter how famous or how big a star—had to pass through metal detectors like those at airports. The producers of the Oscar presentations were taking no chances.

One of the first stars to arrive was Whoopi Goldberg, who brought her teenage daughter, Alexandrea. Goldberg was one of the five women competing in the category of Best Supporting Actress. She had been nominated for her performance in the movie *Ghost*, in which she portrays Oda Mae Brown, a woman who claims she can communicate with people who have died.

Oda Mae is a fake. She pretends she can talk to the dead as a way of getting money from people. However, she is in for a huge surprise when she discovers that she really *can* communicate with a dead person—Sam. In the beginning of the film, Sam (played by Patrick Swayze) is killed by a robber. As a ghost, he tries to get Oda Mae to give a message to his girlfriend, Molly (played by Demi Moore).

Whoopi Goldberg and Demi Moore in *Ghost.*

Ghost was one of the biggest hits of 1990. Not all movie critics liked the film, but the public liked it, and many critics had high praise for Whoopi Goldberg's performance. The critic for *The New York Times* thought Goldberg was excellent in the part of Oda Mae. She wrote, "Ms. Goldberg has found a film role that really suits her, and she makes the most of it."[1] The critic for the *Los Angeles Times* called Goldberg "wickedly funny."[2] Another critic liked her performance so much that he called it the best acting in the film.[3] Goldberg's performance was so well received that many people thought she was going to win the Oscar that night.

When movie stars arrive at the Oscar ceremony, they walk down a red carpet that has been unrolled on the street outside the auditorium, and they are often interviewed before they go inside. As Goldberg and her daughter walked down the carpet, gossip columnist Cindy Adams and other reporters waited for them. Adams asked Goldberg how she felt. Goldberg told her that if the predictions were correct and she did win the Oscar, "Boy, will I celebrate. But the first thing I'll do to celebrate is to take off these . . . shoes."[4]

That remark was typical of Goldberg, who is known for saying exactly what is on her mind. Her honesty sometimes offends people, but many others respect her for being straightforward and down-to-earth.

Goldberg might have been many people's choice to win the Academy Award that night, but nothing was certain. First, no black woman had won an Oscar in more than fifty years. Hattie McDaniel, who played Scarlet O'Hara's "Mammy" in *Gone With the Wind*, won the 1939 Best Supporting Actress Oscar. McDaniel was the first black person ever to be nominated for an Academy Award, and only three black actors had won Oscars since McDaniel (Sidney Poitier, 1963; Louis Gosset, Jr., 1982; Denzel Washington, 1989).

Second, Goldberg had been nominated for an Oscar in the category of Best Actress for her performance in the 1985 film *The Color Purple*. But she did not win that year. She made several other films after *The Color Purple*, but they were not as successful as that movie.

Ghost, however, was very successful. It was the second-highest-grossing film of 1990, earning more than $200 million in that year. So Whoopi Goldberg was waiting again . . . waiting to learn whether she would win the Oscar this time.

Win or lose, she would not have to wait long. The Oscar for Best Supporting Actress was the first award that would be given. The ceremonies began with an opening speech by the president of the Academy of Motion Pictures Arts and Sciences, the organization that gives out the Oscars. Then, comedian Billy Crystal, the evening's host, performed a monologue and told jokes about the movie industry.

The ceremony had been going on for twenty-two

minutes when the moment arrived. Onstage, Denzel Washington, who had won the 1989 Best Supporting Actor Oscar for his performance in *Glory*, read the names of the nominees: Annette Bening for *The Grifters*, Lorraine Bracco for *Goodfellas*, Whoopi Goldberg for *Ghost*, Diane Ladd for *Wild at Heart*, Mary McDonnell for *Dances with Wolves*. As each name was read, the camera cut to the actress, sitting in the auditorium.

The audience was quiet. Denzel Washington broke the seal on the envelope that held the name of the winner. He tore the envelope open. Then he read the name of the best supporting actress of 1990.

"Whoopi Goldberg!"

Everyone burst into applause. The orchestra played "Unchained Melody," the song featured in *Ghost*. Goldberg kissed her daughter, then rose and walked to the stage. Her black sequined gown shimmered in the television lights.

When Washington held out the Oscar, Goldberg hesitated before taking it. Then she turned to the audience to make her acceptance speech. Millions of people all over the world were watching. "Ever since I was a little kid, I wanted this," she said. "My brother's sitting there and he's saying, 'Thank God we don't have to listen to that anymore.'"[5]

Next, she thanked her *Ghost* costar Patrick Swayze for helping her to get the role of Oda Mae Brown.

Then, choking back tears, Goldberg said to those in the auditorium, "I come from New York. When I was a little kid, I lived in the projects. You're the people I watched; the people I wanted to be. I'm proud to be an actor."[6]

Afterward Goldberg went backstage, where reporters were waiting to ask her questions. But first she did exactly what she had told Cindy Adams she would do: She kicked off her shoes. The reporters asked how it felt to win the Oscar. She said that when Denzel Washington named her as the winner, "Words, bad words, were forming in my mouth. . . . Then I remembered where I was."[7]

In 1990, in addition to appearing in *Ghost*, Goldberg appeared in another film, *The Long Walk Home*. This movie is about how black people were treated in the South during the 1950s. Reporters wanted to know whether Goldberg was sorry she had won for her comedic role in *Ghost* rather than for the serious film. "Are you kidding? I'm thrilled," she told them.[8]

She also had other things to say. "I never say I'm black (when I'm looking for work) . . . because as soon as you say it, they tell you there's no work for you. You wouldn't say to a doctor that he couldn't operate on your kneecap because he is black. In the same way, art should have no color."[9]

Ghost was Goldberg's tenth film. It would make her a major star, and she would go on to be one of the

"Ever since I was a little kid, I wanted this," said Whoopi Goldberg when she won an Academy Award for her performance in *Ghost.*

highest-paid actresses in Hollywood. There would also be many other honors to come.

But tonight was a special triumph all its own. Whoopi Goldberg, the first black actress to win an Oscar in fifty-one years, had indeed come a very long way since she lived in the projects in New York City.

2

GROWING UP IN NEW YORK

hoopi Goldberg was born Caryn Johnson on November 13, 1955, in New York City. Years later, her mother would tell her it seemed as if she started performing the minute she was born. "I immediately put my thumb in my mouth," Goldberg has said. "Doctors were calling nurses to come over and look at this very odd baby who came out sort of ready to start. . . . My mom said she knew then that I was probably going to be an entertainer of some kind."[1]

Caryn's father, Robert Johnson, abandoned the family when she was a baby. She and her brother, Clyde, who was six years older, were raised by their mother. Emma Johnson was a nurse and, later, a preschool teacher in a program called Head Start.

Goldberg remembers her childhood as being a happy one. "We were partners, growing up. It was just me and my mother and Clyde, in our little apartment in Chelsea. We all looked out for each other," she has said.[2] The family did not have much money, but Emma Johnson made sure her children got the things that really mattered. There was always enough food in the house, and she was always ready with a hug when her children needed one.

Goldberg grew up in the Eliot-Chelsea housing project, at Tenth Avenue and Twenty-sixth Street, in a working-class city neighborhood named Chelsea. Goldberg has described it as "a neighborhood full of blacks, whites, Greeks, Jews, Puerto Ricans, and Italians. You had to speak a smattering of all the languages, 'cause you had to ask if your friend was home, and could you stay for dinner."[3]

One of the best times of the year in the Johnson household was Christmas. Every Christmas Eve, Clyde would wake up Caryn in the middle of the night and they would tiptoe into the living room to get an early look at the presents they knew would be under the brightly lit tree. Their apartment had only two rooms and the children had to be very quiet, but somehow they always managed to sneak into the living room undetected. And there, under the tree, were beautifully

As a child, Whoopi Goldberg lived in an apartment here in the Eliot-Chelsea housing projects in New York City. In those days, her name was Caryn Johnson.

wrapped Christmas presents. Caryn and Clyde often wondered how their mother brought so many gifts into the house without being seen, but the children never discovered her secret.

In the summer, the Johnsons went to the amusement park at Coney Island and took boat rides around Manhattan. Mrs. Johnson always urged her children to take advantage of all the culture New York City offers, such as museums and ballet for children. She took Caryn to see films, and she encouraged her to go to young people's concerts and Broadway shows.

Sometimes Caryn did not have to go anywhere to see a show. In the summer, a group called Shakespeare in the Park drove around the city in a truck, visiting different neighborhoods and performing plays on a stage they assembled. The props for the play were kept in the truck, and Goldberg still remembers the neighborhood children watching as the stage was set up. "The truck would be open and magic things would be coming out of it. An hour later, just as the sun was going down, it would be time for the play. It was like the circus coming to town, and on those nights our little neighborhood was the center of the . . . universe."[4]

As a young girl, Caryn was also heavily influenced by the old movies she watched constantly on television. For her, watching these movies was more than just a way to spend free time. She credits them with teaching her about the world and who she could be. She recalls,

"When I watched them, I could be a rich queen living in a foreign country, or I could be a poor girl from the tenements. From movies, I learned you weren't forced to be one person."[5]

She loved the romantic comedies that were made during the 1930s and the horror movies that were made during the 1950s. Her favorite movie stars were Spencer Tracy, Gary Cooper, Jimmy Stewart, Carole Lombard, and Bette Davis. The movie star she liked most of all was John Garfield because she admired his ability to play all kinds of roles, from the romantic hero to the villain.

Caryn did not know it then, but she was doing more than just watching television. She was also learning how to act. While watching old movies, she was seeing how different actors performed. One thing she learned from watching so many actors was that even when they played the same emotion, they showed that feeling in different ways. Caryn realized that there were many ways for an actor to show anger, sadness, happiness, or surprise.

Caryn attended elementary school at the parish school of St. Columbia Church, which was near her home. She describes herself at this time of her life as "the boring child in class—very quiet and shy, but hot-tempered."[6]

When she was eight years old, she discovered that in addition to watching other people perform in theaters and on television, she could perform herself. The Hudson Guild, a neighborhood community center near her home, had a children's group that gave young people the opportunity to act. Caryn became an active member of this group. For her, being allowed to perform was as exciting as being set loose in a candy store to take anything she wanted.[7]

She would later say that acting was all she ever wanted to do. But that dream made her different from her friends. Other children her age were dancing to rock and roll music. Caryn was more interested in the music she had heard at Broadway shows. Because she was interested in different things, Caryn did not always fit in with her friends. There were times when she felt extremely out of place, and this sometimes made her feel lonely.

There were other reasons Caryn did not always fit in. She had trouble reading because she had a learning disability known as dyslexia. (For people who are dyslexic, letters and numbers may appear scrambled or distorted.) And she thought she was too funny-looking to be popular at school. Remembering this part of her childhood, which was not very happy, Goldberg has said, "I was just not a popular girl. I couldn't get a boyfriend. I couldn't get into a clique. I felt I wasn't hip enough or smart enough or fast enough or funny enough or cute enough."[8]

Because she felt she was not popular, Caryn did

Whoopi Goldberg first performed onstage at the Hudson Guild Theatre. She was only eight years old.

things to make people like her. If she and her friends were in the park, and her friends said they wanted candy, Caryn would run off to get candy. But when she came back, her friends would be gone. Caryn's feelings were hurt when this happened, but she so desperately wanted to be liked that the next time her friends said they wanted candy, she would go running off again. And when she came back with the candy, her friends would be gone again.

Caryn attended Washington Irving High School, but she did not stay in school very long. She started using drugs, and during the ninth grade she dropped out of school. As an adolescent she used many different types of drugs. At the age of seventeen she was a heroin addict. Today, Goldberg is very much against drugs and warns young people about the dangers of drugs. She now says, "People [who do drugs] are often looking for some part of themselves. . . . Or they feel small and drugs make them feel big. Sometimes it's a power trip. Sometimes it's just a miniroad to death."[9]

During the 1970s, Caryn participated in civil rights marches and antiwar demonstrations along with many other young people. But the more Caryn did drugs, the more important they became in her life. Finally, she asked herself, "Am I going to keep doing drugs and kill myself or figure out what I'm going to do with my life?"[10] She decided she did not want to be on a miniroad to death. She wanted a life free of drugs. In

1973, she entered a drug treatment program at Horizon House. At Horizon House, she got off drugs and has been off them ever since.

In addition to getting off drugs, Caryn fell in love with her drug counselor, Alvin Martin, and in 1973 they got married. In May 1974, they had a daughter and named her Alexandrea, after Alexander the Great. The marriage did not last very long: Less than two years later, Caryn Johnson and her husband separated.

Now a single mother, Johnson moved back to the projects and lived with her own mother. But the special dream she had as an eight-year-old girl was never far away. As a little girl, Caryn had wanted to be an actor. Now she was determined to pursue that dream, and she focused her energy on getting acting roles. She went to auditions. She tried to meet people who hired actors. However, like most struggling actors, she spent more time looking for roles than actually performing.

Several weeks after moving back to the projects to live with her mother, Johnson faced another big decision about what to do with her life. A friend she knew from the theater asked her to leave New York City with him.

3

A NEW LIFE IN CALIFORNIA

ohnson's friend was moving to Lubbock, Texas. He had a one-year-old child, and he asked Johnson to go with him and take care of his child. Alexandrea was also a year old, and Johnson liked taking care of children, so she decided to go. She said good-bye to New York, and the four of them drove to Texas.

After a while, her friend moved from Texas to San Diego, California. Johnson and Alexandrea went, too, but in California Johnson and her friend went their separate ways. Johnson found herself in San Diego with no job and no way to get back to New York.

Over the next several years, she worked at many

different jobs to support herself and her daughter. She worked as a bricklayer, learned to do masonry, and worked in a bank. She was a model for the Deloux School of Beauty, where she let students work on her hair. After a while, she began to think about becoming a hairstylist herself, but she could not afford to pay for training. Fortunately, the man who ran the school believed in helping people, and Johnson was given a scholarship. After sixteen hundred hours of training, she became a certified cosmetologist (a person specially trained to style hair and apply makeup). Johnson worked as a hairstylist for a while. Then she got a job in a funeral home, where she did the hair of dead people to help prepare them for burial.

Working in a funeral home was sometimes difficult. Johnson made it easier for herself by imagining that the dead people she worked on were large dolls. Thinking of them as dolls made it easier for her to handle the bodies. No matter how difficult this work was, Johnson was determined to keep her job because she had to support her daughter. She also learned to find humor in her work. "It was . . . much better than working on live people . . . they never complained about how they looked," she has joked.[1]

Johnson had not given up her dream of being a performer. The friend she had gone to San Diego with introduced her to people at the San Diego Repertory Company, and she began to work with them.

Sometimes she did actors' hair or makeup. Sometimes she would act in a play. When she got paid for her theater work, she would earn $25 per show.

Johnson was working at several jobs, but they did not bring in enough money to live on. So she turned to welfare. When she earned money from working, she was honest and reported the income to the people at the welfare office. They would then subtract that amount from her next welfare check. But by the time Johnson got her welfare check, the money she had earned elsewhere was long gone. When it came to matters of money, these were difficult times for Caryn Johnson and her daughter.

Johnson continued working with the San Diego Repertory Company, and she also joined an improvisational group called Spontaneous Combustion. Improvisational groups do not use a script when they perform. Instead of memorizing their lines, they make up the show as they go along.

As in New York, getting work as an actor was difficult. There were many actors, but only a few roles. And Johnson faced another problem—race. There were very few black actors in San Diego, and many of the plays being performed were originally written for white people. Johnson was willing to take any part, but most of the time the producers of the plays did not want to hire a black actor to perform with a white actor. They told Johnson that audiences would not accept it.

They were worried that seeing her onstage with a white actor might shock some audiences so much that people would stop coming to see the play. Still, these same producers who would not hire her also told her that they thought she was a good actor.

So Johnson went in a new creative direction that would affect her career as a performer and her life as an artist. She started performing comedy in small clubs. She had not planned to do comedy, but she discovered that she had a real talent for making people laugh. In addition, instead of waiting for people to hire her to portray a character someone else had written, she started to develop her own characters. In doing this, she created work for herself and gained more control over the type of acting she did.

After a while, she began to use these characters in sketches as part of her act. She called her characters "spooks," and each night she performed them a little differently, depending on how the audience reacted. One of her new characters was a drug addict named Fontaine. Another was a black girl who wished that she were white. Another was a teenage girl who got pregnant and gave herself an abortion.

Sometimes Johnson's spooks upset people. A group offended by her sketch on teenage abortion picketed her show and sent her threatening letters. But she refused to stop performing this sketch. Rather than

In the early days of her career, Goldberg discovered her gift for making people laugh.

give in and change her show, she thanked the protesters for giving her free publicity.

Performing comedy and creating her own characters were two important changes in Johnson's early career. Another important change was a new name. It was in San Diego that Caryn Johnson became Whoopi Goldberg. She recalls that a friend said, "'If I was your mother, I would have called you Whoopi, because when you're unhappy you make a sound like a whoopee cushion.' . . . So people actually started calling me Whoopi Cushion."[2]

The name was silly, but it was meant to be funny. For a while, she also tried making it sound French, by calling herself Whoopi Cush-on. But her mother was worried about her new name. Emma Johnson thought her daughter would not be taken seriously with a name like Whoopi Cushion. When her daughter insisted on keeping Whoopi as a first name, Mrs. Johnson suggested she use Goldberg as a last name.

For many years Whoopi Goldberg refused to reveal where her new last name came from, saying only that it was from somewhere in her family history. Over the years, she has told different stories about how she chose her last name. Sometimes she said it was the name of a distant relative. Sometimes she joked that a voice coming from a burning bush told her to call herself Whoopi Goldberg.

It is common to hear or read different versions of

events in Goldberg's early life and career. For many years, she said she was born in 1949, deliberately making herself older. As a struggling actor trying to get work, she sometimes claimed to have done things that cannot be proved. Goldberg has since said she changed some information about herself so people would hire her. She felt that if people thought she were older, or had done certain kinds of work, or had certain kinds of training, they would be more likely to hire her for their shows. One reason she changed her name was that she hoped an unusual name would be easily remembered by casting directors, the people who hire actors.

Whoopi Goldberg was such an unusual name that it often gave audiences the wrong impression. People who did not know who this performer was thought they were going to see someone Jewish. They certainly did not expect to see a black performer onstage. But over the years, Goldberg found that the name had certain advantages. "Once they get past the fact that I'm Whoopi Goldberg," she has said, "then they realize anything is possible."[3]

In the late 1970s, Goldberg met Don Victor, a comedian, and they decided to perform together as a team. Calling themselves Victor and Goldberg, they did improvisational comedy in small clubs around San Diego.

Toward the end of 1980, the Hawkeyes, a theater group from Berkeley, California, came to San Diego and taught acting workshops. Goldberg attended one of the workshops. She liked the type of work the Hawkeyes did and invited them to see her and Victor perform. When the Hawkeyes saw the two comedians, they liked their show and invited them to perform in Berkeley, which is across the bay from San Francisco.

Goldberg and Victor accepted the invitation to perform in Berkeley, but the night before they had to fly there, Victor got sick and could not make the trip. So Goldberg flew to San Francisco by herself.

One of the Hawkeyes, David Schein, met her at the airport. Goldberg apologized for being alone and explained that Victor had been unable to come with her. Schein told her, "Just do what you do when you work with Don and make the audience your partner. What's the worst that can happen? You do twenty minutes, and, if you're bad, you'll know it and you'll get off the stage."[4]

When Goldberg got to the club, she decided to go onstage and talk very fast, so the audience would not see how inexperienced she was at performing alone. When she finished her act, she was in for a big surprise. She remembers, "People got up and stamped their feet and screamed and hollered and carried on."[5] Goldberg saw that she could go onstage alone, perform her characters, and be a success. From that night on, she would continue to perform her spooks as a solo artist.

In the summer of 1981, Goldberg and Alexandrea

left San Diego and moved to Berkeley. Goldberg was still on welfare, but now she was in love with David Schein, who was helping her take care of Alexandrea. Schein encouraged her to develop her act. A few years later Goldberg described this period as a time when her life started to get better.

Now that she was living in Berkeley, Goldberg became part of the Hawkeyes. She also continued to work on her spooks and to develop new characters, until she had thirteen. Her characters included a heroin addict, a surfer girl, and a burglar. These characters slowly evolved into *The Spook Show*. Goldberg first performed *The Spook Show* in the fall of 1982, at the Hawkeye Theater in Berkeley. The critic for the *San Francisco Chronicle* had high praise for Goldberg's skill at comedy and her talent for portraying many different characters with great accuracy.

As she began to work in other theaters around San Francisco, Goldberg developed her ability to deal with different kinds of audiences. At the Hawkeye Theater, the audiences were respectful and listened to performances quietly. But at other places, audiences could be noisy. One night, when Goldberg was performing at a club called the Valencia Rose, people started calling things out to her while she was onstage. Some performers would have ignored this, but Goldberg responded by involving the audience in her performance. She even stepped off the stage, went to

Playing many different characters helped Goldberg sharpen her acting skills.

different tables in the club, and talked directly to the people seated at the tables.

In the fall of 1983, Goldberg worked with director Ellen Sebastian to create a new show, *Moms*. Goldberg played Moms Mabley, a black comedian who became a star with black audiences during the 1920s. Mabley was also the first black woman comedian known to white audiences, and her comedy records became extremely popular in the 1960s. Moms Mabley performed without teeth, wearing a housecoat, a nightcap, colorful socks, and oversize shoes.

Moms opened on October 12, 1983, at the Hawkeye Theater. The *San Francisco Chronicle* critic who had liked *The Spook Show* so much also liked Goldberg's new show. *Moms* later earned Goldberg her first award as a professional actor: a Bay Area Critics' Award.

In the fall of 1983, Goldberg also returned to San Diego to perform at the Old Globe Theater. Her old friends were amazed at how good she had become. One of them said, "She had honed her acting skills with the Hawkeyes, and she could twist the audience around her little finger. You could hear a pin drop. At that point we thought, 'She's going to make it.'"[6]

4

BACK TO NEW YORK

s Goldberg performed throughout the San Francisco area, more people became familiar with her work. In New York City, David White, who ran the Dance Theater Workshop, heard about her from a friend in San Francisco. White was looking for new talent and invited Goldberg to New York to perform *The Spook Show* at the Dance Theater Workshop.

Goldberg believed in herself, but she was not sure whether she was ready to perform in New York. She decided to go because it was also a chance to see her mother. When the people at the theater asked for a photograph of her, she imagined that "they wanted my picture so they could put an arrow on it and say, 'Don't see her, she stinks.'" [1]

The Spook Show did not have costumes or scenery. Goldberg performed alone on a bare stage. She used her voice, her body, different accents, and different ways of moving to create each character. Sometimes she would put something on her head, like a scarf, a hat, or a shirt. When she wanted to become a new character, she would turn around and adjust her body and voice. Then, when she faced the audience again, she would be someone else.

One of Goldberg's spooks is a young black girl who wants to be white and have blond hair. To give herself blond hair, Goldberg wears a shirt on her head. Years later, Goldberg revealed that this little girl was inspired by Alexandrea. Another spook is a drug addict named Fontaine who goes to Europe and visits the house in Amsterdam where Anne Frank and her family hid from the Nazis for two years. Another character is a disabled woman. Goldberg told an interviewer that this spook was created for some wheelchair-bound friends in Berkeley who asked her to write material about what it was like to be disabled. When Goldberg told her friends that she did not want to make fun of them, they said, "But this is funny stuff! Some of us look funny! . . . but *inside* we're just like anybody else. Physically we're a little different but so what? If you could just get people to stop talking to us like babies, or talking to us like we're deaf, we'd be so happy."[2] Goldberg has said this character became her favorite because she is so gentle and understands other people so well.

People often asked Goldberg how she developed her spooks. She has said that she did not write her sketches down, as many performers do. Instead, she created characters by thinking about them a great deal. Wherever she went, she was always observing people and looking at what was going on around her. Sometimes she remembered small details about what someone looked like or what someone did. Sometimes people told her interesting stories. When she saw someone or heard something that she thought would fit into her act, she developed it into a sketch for one of her characters. When she believed the sketch was ready to be seen, she performed it for audiences, reworking it a little each time until it expressed exactly what she was trying to say.

Goldberg opened *The Spook Show* at the Dance Theater Workshop on January 27, 1984. She had been afraid she would be a failure, but she could not have been more wrong. Just as when she first went onstage solo in San Francisco, audiences loved what she did.

At first, however, not many people came to see the show because no one knew who this new performer was. Then, a critic from *The New York Times* came to the theater. After seeing this unknown performer, he wrote a very enthusiastic review in which he called Goldberg "a fresh and very funny character comedian."[3]

The Dance Theater Workshop is a small theater located up two flights of stairs in a building that was originally a garage. The review in *The New York Times* brought people to the show, and the following Saturday night a crowd was lined up on the staircase leading to the theater. Those in line were black and white, and included college students in jeans, well-dressed middle-aged men, and older women wearing furs. Goldberg's show was attracting everyone. By the time the show began, people were even sitting on the floor.

Some audience members were highly entertained by *The Spook Show*. Others were troubled or offended. But Goldberg has often pointed out that when she performs onstage, she tries to do more than just make people laugh. She believes that one reason people come to see her is to be surprised by what she does in her show—and she tries to do more than simply entertain her audiences. She has said, "I want to make people laugh and *think*."[4]

In addition to being a success, Goldberg had another important experience in New York. The Dance Theater Workshop is in Chelsea, just a few blocks from the housing project where she grew up. She decided to go back to see some of the people from her childhood. She especially wanted to see people who had made fun of her when she was young. They had

The Dance Theater Workshop, in New York City, is on the second floor of a building that used to be a garage. After Goldberg performed *The Spook Show* here, her career began to take off.

laughed at her. Now that she was starting to succeed, she wanted to somehow get even with them.

But when Goldberg returned to her old neighborhood, things were not as she expected them to be. She discovered that many of those who had made fun of her when she was young had not moved forward with their lives, as she had. Some of them were not even familiar with the world that lay beyond their neighborhood. Instead of getting back at these people, she thought about how lucky she was. She later said that she was glad she had been so different from her friends. Being different gave her different dreams. Those dreams gave her the motivation to move beyond her childhood neighborhood and make a new life for herself.

She was still different, but now people were praising her for it, not making fun of her. At the theater she was applauded by her audiences, and after the show other performers came backstage to say how much they admired her. One of these was an important director, Mike Nichols, who had made the films *The Graduate* and *Catch-22*. He too was once a comedian and was so impressed with Goldberg that he offered to produce her show on Broadway. Goldberg did not think he was serious. When he came backstage, they talked about the shows they were working on. After he left her dressing room, Goldberg did not expect to hear from him again.

At last Whoopi Goldberg was getting noticed. She was getting attention. She was getting offers. But it was all going too fast. So she returned to what was familiar—to her family and friends in Berkeley.

In San Francisco, she performed *Moms* again. But this time the theater was larger and people arrived in limousines. Goldberg had moved beyond tiny nightclubs and small theaters. Her audiences were getting bigger. Her career was taking off. Her entire life was changing.

One of the most important changes in her life was that after seven years of being on welfare, Goldberg was finally able to support herself and her daughter on her own. When she received her next welfare check, she sent it back to the welfare office. But she decided to save her welfare identification card. She framed it to remind herself of those difficult years when she had struggled so hard.

Goldberg had gotten off welfare. She had scored a big success in New York, which brought her national recognition and enabled her to sign a contract with a talent manager who would guide her career. People were offering her work. "I kinda feel like I'm on the brink of something, in the eye of a hurricane," she told an interviewer. "It's real nice and it's real awful, too. . . . All this stuff is coming to me on a silver platter. . . . People literally have told me, 'Anything you want, ask.'"[5]

There was one thing she did not even have to ask

for: Mike Nichols sent a letter to her in Berkeley saying that he still wanted to produce her show on Broadway. It was an opportunity that could transform her career. But she later revealed that she almost said no. Goldberg was not sure what effect going to New York might have on her family. She knew that her family did not want to move to New York, and she said that if they told her not to go, she would have stayed in Berkeley.

She drove to Vermont with Alexandrea and David Schein to take a vacation and think things over. Then she said yes.

Whoopi Goldberg was on her way to Broadway.

5

BACK TO
BROADWAY

lexandrea, who was now nine, returned to Berkeley with Schein, and Goldberg went to New York. If she did as well in a big Broadway theater as she had done at the small Dance Theater Workshop, she would be a star.

While she was preparing for the show, Goldberg talked to a reporter for *Interview* magazine about what it felt like to be famous. She said that what she liked most about her new status was that the money she was earning gave her the freedom to enjoy the simple things of everyday life. She could now buy groceries and pay her rent and pay her phone bills. When she went shopping for clothes, she could now afford to buy several pairs of pants at a time. When she traveled, she could now stay at nicer, more interesting places. She said, "It's like a dream, and I feel like I'm living it for so many people—my mom, my family and my friends."[1]

Goldberg was not very famous yet. But she was already discovering that being a celebrity could create problems as well as make life better. She compared being famous to trying to walk through a minefield. She also talked about the fact that when little-known performers become celebrities, people who ignored them before they were famous suddenly want to be their friends.

Mike Nichols directed Goldberg in her Broadway show, which was called *Whoopi Goldberg* and opened at the Lyceum Theater on October 24, 1984. By now she had developed seventeen spooks, and in this show she performed six of them: Fontaine the drug addict and thief; the Valley Girl surfer chick; the little black girl who wants to be white; a Jamaican woman who marries a rich older American man; the disabled woman; and a has-been tap dancer.

Opening night is a tense time for performers, and it is a Broadway tradition to go to Sardi's restaurant to wait for the newspaper reviews to be published. Goldberg went to Sardi's, but she decided not to read the reviews of her show. She had already heard that they were not all good. If a show gets enough bad reviews, it will close. She knew this could happen to

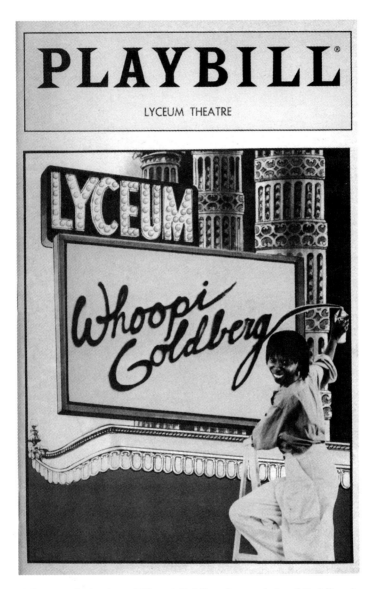

The Broadway show *Whoopi Goldberg* featured six of Goldberg's characters, including the drug addict Fontaine and a disabled woman. "I want to make people laugh and *think*," Goldberg has said.

her show and was prepared to face that possibility. She felt that if *Whoopi Goldberg* did close because of bad reviews, her life would not be over and neither would her career. She would just go home to Berkeley and continue to perform in nightclubs and small theaters.

The critic for the *New York Post* liked the show very much, writing that Goldberg "seems to have everything going for her—including a quite sizable talent and a more than sizable nerve."[2] The *Village Voice* called Goldberg "one of the great actors of her generation."[3] There were also negative reviews of the show, but many of the critics who did not like the show still praised Goldberg's talent.

Even though *Whoopi Goldberg* received bad reviews as well as good ones, people went to see the show and it was a success. Soon Goldberg was being called "the toast of Broadway." She was acknowledged and praised by Broadway professionals and by theater audiences. Some people loved the show, some did not like it at all, and some people were disappointed because they thought Goldberg should have aimed her show at black people. Goldberg responded to this by saying, "The art of acting is not a Black or White art. It's not supposed to be. . . . But because of the way things have developed over the last four hundred years, everything is segregated. Which is awful."[4]

The theater kept selling out. And, as at the Dance Theater Workshop, the audience included celebrities.

One night, country-music star Dolly Parton came to see the show. The audience could not seem to decide whether to look at Goldberg or at Parton. Many performers would have been bothered by this, but for Goldberg it just added to the excitement of the evening.

Only a few months earlier, Goldberg had been a struggling performer waiting for her big break. She had many friends who were still waiting for their break, and she ended her show by acknowledging other struggling performers. After each show, she returned to the stage, talked about how grateful she was, and reminded people that other artists all over the country were trying to succeed. She was not saying this to impress audiences. Goldberg was happy that she was finally being recognized, but she was also keenly aware that she was one of the lucky ones. She had worked hard to get to this point in her career, and she felt she had earned her success. Yet she was also quick to point out that there were many other artists who were as talented as she was but who had not had her luck.

For Goldberg, one of the big thrills of her new fame came from a cartoon. Waiting for reviews at Sardi's is one Broadway tradition. Another tradition is that when a show opens, *The New York Times* asks the artist Abe Hirschfeld to draw a caricature of the people in the show. Hirschfeld likes to include his daughter Nina's name in his drawings, often hiding the letters of her name in people's hair or clothing. Like many New

Yorkers, Goldberg grew up looking for the hidden "Ninas" in Hirschfeld's drawings. Now *she* was in a Hirschfeld drawing.

Hirschfeld drew five characters from Goldberg's show and put forty "Ninas" in the drawing. Goldberg was elated. Hirschfeld had come to the theater twice to study her for the caricatures. For Goldberg, getting forty "Ninas" was especially pleasing. She was so thrilled that she sent Hirschfeld flowers.

All her life Goldberg had admired movie stars and performers. Now she was a rising star, but she still felt like a fan. One of the most exciting things for her was the fact that she could now say she would like to meet some famous performer and before she knew it, she was actually meeting that person. She was introduced to celebrities like Jack Nicholson, Jane Fonda, Dustin Hoffman, Glenn Close, Lily Tomlin, William Hurt, and Michael Jackson. She said, "I feel like I'm living in a dream. I'm the worst. I gawk. My mouth gets dry. My ears move."[5]

Every show closes eventually, and Goldberg began to talk about what she wanted to do after *Whoopi Goldberg* closed. She mentioned other parts she wanted to play onstage. These roles had not been played by black actors before. She knew that the idea of a black woman in a role written for a white person was hard for some people to accept. She had been told this since her days in San Diego. But she believed she could

The Lyceum Theater, above, kept selling out for Whoopi Goldberg's Broadway show, and Goldberg was thrilled with the enthusiasm of her audiences.

change people's attitudes. She believed that her talent, and her ability to play any part, would bring her the roles she wanted.

Besides performing, Goldberg had always been involved with social issues. Now she was in a position to use her fame to support the causes she believed in. After her show closed, she went to New York's Cathedral of St. John the Divine as a guest speaker for the cathedral's Lenten series on the homeless. She talked for ten minutes, asking the seven thousand people who came to worship to help the homeless in any way they could.

In November 1984, *Esquire* magazine named thirty-one young northern Californians as the "best of the new generation," calling them "achievers who are changing America."[6] Whoopi Goldberg was on the list.

Goldberg's new status would help her get parts. It would give more importance to her words when she spoke out for the things she believed in. But fame could also mean getting too much attention. As a hot new talent, and someone who was determined to dress as she pleased and say whatever she wanted, Goldberg became a favorite subject in the press. Magazines wrote about everything she did. They kept asking what her real name was, but she refused to reveal it. When reporters asked why she was being so secretive, she told them she wanted to keep her family out of the public spotlight. She also wanted to protect her own privacy and not be treated like a celebrity all the time.

Her new fame was affecting her life in other ways, too. As Goldberg would often point out, it can be very hard to maintain a relationship when the press is always watching. After her Broadway show closed she returned to Berkeley, but her life was no longer quite the same. There was tension in her relationship with Schein. They began to drift apart, and their romantic involvement eventually came to an end.

Goldberg knew that fame can come quickly but be gone quickly, too. She was prepared for this to happen to her. She told one reporter that "in this business . . . you can one day be the toast of Broadway and the next be dried bread. But it won't hurt me. I can walk into any little theater in this country or around the world and just do my show. That's peace of mind."[7]

Getting forty "Ninas" had thrilled Goldberg. Another cartoon also made her feel proud. Just as she had looked at Hirschfeld's cartoons as a child, she had also read *Mad* magazine. One day Alexandrea showed her an issue of *Mad* magazine that would come to mean something very special to Goldberg. *Mad* had done a parody of the movie *Beverly Hills Cop*, and one of the panels showed Goldberg with the label "Valley Girl" (one of her spooks). "It was a *big* deal to me," Goldberg remembers.[8]

Being parodied in *Mad* magazine *was* a big deal: Whoopi Goldberg was a star!

6

WHOOPI GOLDBERG: FILM STAR

fter the success of her Broadway show, Goldberg was getting offers to do films. There was one role she really wanted. A movie was being made of Alice Walker's novel *The Color Purple*. Goldberg had wanted to play a part in this film ever since she and her daughter had heard Walker read from *The Color Purple* on the radio while they were driving around Berkeley. Years later, Goldberg recalled, "Alexandrea said: 'She sounds just like you, Mom, talking to God.' I'm only aware of God whenever I see Baryshnikov dance or a painting or a great actor, or writing like Alice's. So I wrote Alice a fan letter."[1]

Goldberg told Walker how much she liked *The Color*

Purple and expressed her interest in playing a part in the film. In her letter, she wrote, "You don't know me but my name is Whoopi, and here's all my reviews from the Bay Area. . . . I just read *The Color Purple*, and if there's a movie . . . I'd be dirt on the floor, I'd do anything."[2] Walker wrote back, saying that she not only knew who Goldberg was, but that she often went to her shows and had already talked about her to people who were involved with making *The Color Purple* into a film.

Several months later, Goldberg was in Los Angeles when she was contacted by an important director for the second time. It was Steven Spielberg, director of *Jaws* and *E.T.* He had never seen Goldberg perform, and he asked her to come to his private screening room and perform for him and a few of his friends. When she got to the screening room, Goldberg discovered that these friends included Michael Jackson, Quincy Jones, Alice Walker, and the singers Ashford and Simpson.

Goldberg performed her show as if she were doing it in a regular theater. But she decided to add a sketch that people had told her not to do. This sketch was a parody of the movie *E.T.* In Goldberg's parody, E.T. is arrested and put in jail.

People had warned Goldberg not to do this sketch because it might offend Spielberg. But the opposite happened. Spielberg thought the sketch was very funny. After Goldberg performed her show, Spielberg told her that he was thinking about making a film of *The Color Purple* and he wanted to give her a part.

Spielberg offered Goldberg the role of Celie, the film's central character. Goldberg had been thinking that playing Sofia, one of the other characters, would be a good way to begin her film career. Now she was being offered a much bigger role. She started to tell Spielberg that she was not sure what she wanted to do. "And then I realized that Steven Spielberg's sitting there trying to convince me to be in his movie. And it was like, 'Wake up, stupid. Say yes.'"[3]

Goldberg liked working with Spielberg. She respected him as a director, and he helped her make the adjustment from acting onstage to acting in films. She said that Spielberg told her to imagine there were millions of silent people in the camera and they were all looking at her. "He would say, 'They're all in one room looking through a one-way mirror; you can't see them but they can see you. They're mute, so you can't hear them but they hear you, and they enjoy what you're doing.' And that's how the camera became my friend."[4]

While working on *The Color Purple*, Goldberg and Spielberg discovered they had a special way of communicating with each other because they both love films. When he wanted her to act a certain way, he would mention a scene from a movie they both knew and Goldberg would immediately understand exactly how he wanted her to act.

The dinner-table scene in *The Color Purple* had special significance for Goldberg because her daughter, Alexandrea, has a part in it. (She is the laughing child sitting next to Oprah Winfrey.) This scene was special for another reason as well. It was Goldberg's hardest scene in the movie. Before filming this scene, she had been thinking a great deal about Celie's character. She was especially intrigued by how quiet Celie is all the time. When she did the dinner-table scene, Goldberg gained a better understanding of Celie's character and of the entire film. She realized *The Color Purple* is not just a film about black people. It is a story about how powerful love can be.

The Color Purple was released in December 1985. Not everyone liked the film, and the response to Goldberg's performance was mixed. But several reviewers had high praise for Goldberg's work in her first movie.

Whoopi Goldberg was now a full-fledged movie star. Caught up in the excitement of the movie industry, she was going to countless parties, openings, benefits, and other events. She seemed to be everywhere, and the press was always waiting for her. But Goldberg did not act like a star. She was still thrilled when she met other film stars. She still wore her hair in the long, elaborate dreadlocks that had become her

Whoopi Goldberg played the character Celie in *The Color Purple*, directed by Steven Spielberg.

trademark. She still dressed as she had always dressed, usually in baggy clothes or jeans, and she often wore sneakers. She still said whatever was on her mind and did what she pleased instead of what she was expected to do. *People* magazine named her one of the most intriguing people of 1985.

But some reporters began to treat Goldberg as a joke. Years later, she responded to this, saying, "Someone even wrote that I'd go to the opening of an envelope. That hurt very deeply. I guess no one realized how new all of this was to me."[5] The people who were making jokes about her seemed to forget that although Goldberg was now a celebrity, she still remembered her years of poverty and struggling. She considered it an honor to meet the people she had idolized when she was growing up in a New York City housing project.

Goldberg's determination to be her own person was clearly demonstrated during a 1985 photo shoot. At the time she was wearing a retainer because she had gotten her wisdom teeth removed and her other teeth had started moving. The photographer was about to take her picture, when Goldberg stopped because her retainer was not in her mouth. Her press agent did not want her to wear the retainer for the picture, but Goldberg popped it into her mouth and said, "Why not? People should see it. It's real."[6]

She also stayed in touch with her friends in

Berkeley who knew her before she became famous. She knew she could rely on them to remind her who she really was if she started acting like a star when she was with them. After all, these were the same people who had given her rides to the welfare office. Goldberg knew that a famous person's ego can become too big, and she did not want that to happen to her.

When the 1985 Oscar nominations were announced, Goldberg was nominated for Best Actress, and her *Color Purple* costars Margaret Avery and Oprah Winfrey were nominated in the category of Best Supporting Actress. It was the first time three black women received Oscar nominations in the same year. If Goldberg won, she would become the first black woman to win the Oscar for Best Actress.

But Goldberg did not think she would win. She told reporters she felt it was not the right time for her to win an Academy Award. She joked that if Meryl Streep's husband, the artist Donald Gummer, sculpted an Oscar for her, that would be as good as winning the real thing.

Goldberg did not win the Oscar, though she did receive other awards for her performance in *The Color Purple*, including the Golden Globe Award for Best Performance by an Actress. She also won a 1985 Grammy Award (the music industry's equivalent of the Oscar) for Best Comedy Recording, for the album of

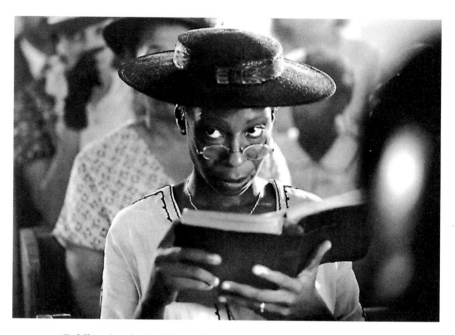

Goldberg's role in *The Color Purple* brought her a 1985 Oscar nomination for Best Actress.

her Broadway show, *Whoopi Goldberg: Original Broadway Show*.

In 1985, Goldberg also received a very special award that had nothing to do with show business. The University of Charleston in West Virginia gave her an honorary degree. This was quite an honor for a high school dropout who had quit school before finishing the ninth grade.

Still, winning awards that acknowledged her acting talent did not mean that Goldberg could get any role she wanted. After her Broadway show, she had talked hopefully about all the roles she wanted to play. Now she was discovering that getting these parts was not easy. Producers and directors still did not want to cast her in certain roles. Sometimes it was the old problem that people thought in terms of black or white when they cast parts. However, she also faced a new obstacle. She had shown that she could play a dramatic role in *The Color Purple*. But because of her stage work, many people thought of her as a comedian. So those were the kinds of roles they wanted to give her.

And now, having come so far, Goldberg's career was about to take a turn for the worse.

7

A Career
Fades

 oldberg was a star, but she was also a black woman who was thought of as a comic actor. The biggest black comic actor in films at the time was Eddie Murphy, and many movie producers viewed Goldberg as a female Eddie Murphy. They wanted her to play the kinds of characters he did. They wanted her to act the way he did. Those who did not see her this way did not know what kind of acting roles to offer her.

In the black press, some people criticized her for selling out to the mainstream by making a film with Steven Spielberg. They felt she was not being true to herself. Others were upset that a white director had made *The Color Purple,* and still others were angry that Goldberg said Spielberg *should* have made the film.

But Goldberg did not want to be considered a black actress. She was against the idea of labeling someone a black actor or actress, because this kind of narrow thinking limits the roles film producers or casting directors will offer the performer. If a good part is available, but it is thought that it has to be played by a white actor, the filmmakers will not offer it to a black performer, no matter how good the actor is. Goldberg wanted to be considered for any role that she had the ability to play. She told reporters, "I want them to say, 'Oh, here's a great role. Call Meryl Streep. Call Diane Keaton. Call Whoopi Goldberg.'"[1] In fact, Goldberg did not even want to be considered an *actress*. She said, "I am an actor. Actors can do anything. Once you put the 'tress' on the end of it, then you're limited and can't play a male role. I can do anything."[2]

As always, the media were watching to see what outrageous things she would do or say, ready to report on her every move. So much was being published about Goldberg that when a reporter for *Rolling Stone* interviewed her in 1986, he wrote about all the press she was getting. He pointed out that newspapers and magazines were paying extraordinary attention to her. He said that the press had helped to make her a star by writing so many articles about her, but now the same magazines were being too critical of her and accusing her of acting like a star. He also said that Goldberg is a serious person who does not always try to make jokes, and that when he interviewed her, she was extremely down-to-earth and honest.[3]

At this point, Goldberg herself was saying that she might not become a big success in films, and that if she did succeed, it would be because she did not look like a movie star. That was fine with her. She believed that people did not want to keep seeing beautiful faces in films, because most people are not as beautiful as movie stars and know they never will be. Goldberg is not a typical gorgeous star. She looks more like someone you would pass on the street on your way to the store. That was one reason her fans liked her. She said, "What people have told me is that what they like most about me is that I look like I'm from everybody's neighborhood."[4]

Meanwhile, she turned her attention to other interests. In January 1986, she and three friends—Billy Crystal, Robin Williams, and Harold Ramis—founded Comic Relief, an organization to raise money for the homeless. They announced a benefit performance at which the audience could pledge money to help homeless people.

The first Comic Relief show took place on March 30, 1986, at the Universal Amphitheater in Los Angeles. Home Box Office (HBO) made the show available to anyone with basic cable service and did not

In 1986, Goldberg, Robin Williams, Billy Crystal, and Harold Ramis (not pictured) founded Comic Relief to raise money for the homeless.

charge an extra fee for the broadcast. In addition to Goldberg, Crystal, Williams, and Ramis, the performers included Henny Youngman, Martin Short, Pee-wee Herman, Sid Caesar, Carl Reiner, Minnie Pearl, and Michael J. Fox. The show raised a little more than $2 million for the homeless.

While working on Comic Relief, Goldberg met David Edward Claessen, a Dutch documentary filmmaker and cinematographer. A cinematographer is the person in charge of the cameras when a movie is being shot. Goldberg, now legally divorced from her first husband, married Claessen on September 1, 1986, in a small, private ceremony at the Candlelight Wedding Chapel in Las Vegas. To avoid publicity, Goldberg used her real name, Caryn Johnson, on the marriage certificate. The pastor who performed the ceremony thought he recognized Goldberg and asked her if she was an actress. Goldberg smiled, but did not say anything.

In the late 1980s, Goldberg moved to Los Angeles to become more involved with the film industry. Alexandrea, who was now in her teens, stayed in Berkeley and lived with Goldberg's mother, Emma Johnson.

Goldberg's first film after *The Color Purple* was *Jumpin' Jack Flash* (1986). Most critics did not like it. *The New York Times* described it as "her first—and let's hope—her worst motion picture comedy."[5]

Always ready to try something new, Goldberg next tried her hand at reviewing something herself. She loves to read, and one of her favorite authors is Stephen King. When his novel *It* came out, Goldberg reviewed the book for the *Los Angeles Times*.

Her next film was *Burglar* (1987), and once again the critics were negative. In *The New York Times*, the reviewer wrote, "Miss Goldberg is the premier black actress in American films today, but you wouldn't know it from her appearances since *The Color Purple*."[6]

Goldberg was also being criticized by black people who objected to the kind of films she was making. In March 1987, while she was addressing the Black Women's Forum at a Los Angeles hotel, about a dozen blacks demonstrated outside. The spokesperson for the demonstrators said they objected to the bad language Goldberg used when she performed. They thought this language insulted black people. They also said Goldberg was having a bad effect on young blacks.[7]

While making *Burglar*, Goldberg had started wearing blue contact lenses. Some black people accused her of not being "black" enough. True to form, Goldberg did what she wanted. She continued to wear blue contact lenses, and she pointed out that all black people do not have the same color eyes. She enjoyed having blue eyes, and she was not going to let other people tell her what to do.

Goldberg has always been quick to defend herself,

but it especially bothered her that she was being blamed for the roles she was playing. People seemed to think she was deliberately choosing roles that were not up to her talent. They did not understand that she was not offered every role she wanted, and that she did not have control over a film after she agreed to be in it. When an actor finishes performing in a movie, the director often makes changes. Sometimes even the star of the film does not know how the movie has been edited. As for the roles she was playing, Goldberg herself said that she wanted to be in more films like *The Color Purple*, but there were not many movies like that being made and she was not being offered those kinds of roles.

Goldberg was not doing well with the critics, but her fans were still loyal. She continued to perform onstage and was always refining her spooks. Her popularity was growing among younger audiences, so she had Fontaine stop doing drugs. She also used her stage show to try to educate the public about AIDS. In October 1987, talking about some of the changes to her show, she mentioned that the young girl with long hair now had AIDS. She said, "For me, that's the character that gets taken to heart. So, to give her that disease and see how people deal with it—since a lot of smart people are very stupid on this issue—is using humor as a weapon."[8]

Goldberg's next film, *Fatal Beauty* (1987), was an

action-comedy in which she played a detective. She enjoyed all the physical things she got the chance to do while making this film. She said that because it was unusual for a woman to play this kind of role, she felt that *Fatal Beauty* gave her a chance to show the film industry that movies could be cast differently. She hoped it might pave the way for other actors to get roles they would not normally be offered.[9]

But for the third time, the reviews were negative. Even so, audiences were not questioning Goldberg's talent. In January 1988, the California Theater Council honored Goldberg, and January 18 was declared Whoopi Goldberg Day in Los Angeles. Goldberg accepted her award dressed in an orange scarf, black leather pants, and a T-shirt that read "Free South Africa." Then she turned into her character Fontaine and gave her acceptance speech. The event raised $40,000 for a program that encourages non-traditional casting. This means picking the best performer for a role, regardless of the actor's race or gender.

Goldberg's career was apparently being disrupted by a string of bad films. *The Telephone* (1988) received extremely negative reviews. And now her personal life was disrupted as well. On October 4, 1988, Goldberg and David Claessen got divorced.

Clara's Heart (1988) came out the very next day. Reviews were mixed, but this time Goldberg was not being criticized for the roles she was doing. A writer for the *New York Daily News* said that this was her best performance since *The Color Purple*.

As a young girl, Goldberg had watched old movies on TV, and now she was a movie star. She had also watched a lot of television shows, and one of her favorites was *Star Trek*. In 1988, she joined the cast of *Star Trek: The Next Generation*, in the role of Guinan, the psychic bartender.

Gene Roddenberry, *Star Trek*'s producer, was surprised when he learned that Goldberg wanted to be on his show. She was a movie star. He wondered why she would be interested in being in a television series and playing a minor character who did not appear in every episode. But once again, Goldberg had her reasons. As an adult, she was still a huge *Star Trek* fan. When she was a child, *Star Trek* had given her not only pleasure but also hope. She remembered watching the show, seeing the black actress Nichelle Nichols, who plays Lieutenant Uhura, and being joyful to witness a future where black people still existed.

Toward the end of 1989, there was another major change in Goldberg's personal life. Alexandrea, who was fifteen, told Goldberg she was pregnant. Goldberg told her daughter that she did not have to have the baby, but Alexandrea responded that she wanted to have the child. Goldberg did not think her daughter should be a parent at this point in her life, but she was happy that Alexandrea had enough trust in their relationship to come to her and talk about the situation.[10]

Goldberg made her feelings clear to Alexandrea. Then she decided that she would be there for her daughter, whatever Alexandrea decided to do. Ultimately it was Alexandrea's decision, and they were still a family. Like all families, they would have problems. And they would solve them together. Goldberg said, "Just because somebody makes some money and becomes famous doesn't mean the world alters and becomes rosy. People still have lives and problems and all those things that we go through."[11]

The news of Alexandrea's pregnancy appeared on the front pages of the tabloid newspapers. That angered Goldberg very much. *She* was the public figure, not her daughter. If reporters were going to invade her privacy, the stories should be about her, not her family.

Alexandrea gave birth to a baby girl, Amarah Skye Martin, on November 13, 1989—Goldberg's thirty-fourth birthday. Goldberg knew the tabloids were hunting for a picture of her granddaughter, so she took control of the situation. Soon after the baby was born, the Gap clothing stores asked Goldberg to be in some of their ads. Goldberg suggested they take a picture of her, her mother, her daughter, and her granddaughter. She did this because she wanted Amarah's first public picture to be a nice one taken

Whoopi Goldberg, a huge *Star Trek* fan, was happy to play Guinan the psychic bartender in the television show *Star Trek: The Next Generation.*

under pleasant circumstances, rather than a shot snapped by a photographer working for the tabloids. Goldberg also wanted to demonstrate that Alexandrea's family was standing behind her and that they were all there for one another.

In March 1990, Goldberg got her own television series, *Bagdad Cafe*, in which she costarred with the award-winning actress Jean Stapleton. To some people, performing in a television show is a step down from acting in films. There was more talk that Goldberg's career was floundering. But she did not agree. She had always admired Stapleton, and she felt it was an honor to work with her.

By now Comic Relief was an annual show, and *The New York Times* was calling it "one of television's premiere comedy and charity events."[12] Comic Relief IV was broadcast from Radio City Music Hall in New York City. In between rehearsals for the show, Goldberg and Robin Williams went to Washington, D.C., to testify before the Senate Labor and Human Resources Committee. They spoke in support of the Homelessness and Community Revitalization Act, which would provide help for homeless families.

For the past five years, Goldberg had remained true to herself. She took roles she wanted to play, even if other people did not think they were good or right for her. She supported causes she believed in and said what she wanted to say. She was still performing onstage, but her film career had not blossomed and her television series, *Bagdad Cafe*, did not do well. Some people said her career was fading. Some newspaper and magazine writers were saying Goldberg's career was "in the toilet," a show business expression that means failing.

Now that was all about to change.

8

COMEBACK

 oldberg's next film was *The Long Walk Home* (1990), in which she played Odessa, a maid working for a southern white family in the early days of the civil rights movement. With this film Goldberg at last had a good role, and years later she still described *The Long Walk Home* as "some of my best work."[1] The critics agreed.

As Odessa, Goldberg had to remain silent while seeing and hearing many disturbing things. This character was completely different from Goldberg herself. At first the film's director, Richard Pearce, was not sure Goldberg was the right actress for the part. He knew she was quick to speak up about anything to anyone.

But as Odessa, she would have to find other, nonverbal ways to portray her character, and Pearce wondered whether she would be able to do it. Goldberg did more than just play a role. She delivered a performance that pleased Pearce and impressed the critics.

How was Goldberg able to turn herself into Odessa, someone so quiet and passive? Whoopi Goldberg would never remain silent if she were treated the way Odessa was treated. Goldberg thought about the kind of person Odessa was and decided to rely on Odessa's incredible inner strength. No matter what happened, Odessa would not speak up. But she would not let anyone break her spirit.

The Long Walk Home was followed by *Ghost*, and suddenly Goldberg's career had been revived. She was said to be making a comeback. But as far as she was concerned, there was no bad period to come back from. She said, "You read that you're makin' a comeback and you didn't know that you were gone. You read that your career's been in the toilet when you've done seven films back to back. If that's the toilet, my God, let me float forever."[2]

Ghost brought Goldberg her second Oscar nomination, and now she was hot again. She was also learning the rules of the Hollywood game. Yet she was still determined to be the same person she had always been. She was still asking for roles that people did not want to give to a black woman. She still wore her hair

Goldberg described her role as a maid in *The Long Walk Home* as "some of my best work." The officer in this scene was played by actor Haynes Brooke.

in braids when she was not working. She still wore sneakers most of the time. She told an interviewer, "People look at me like a little sister who did real well."[3]

And she would continue to do well. Her TV show, *Bagdad Cafe*, was canceled (the last show was aired on November 23, 1990), but in December Goldberg received two Image Awards from the National Association for the Advancement of Colored People (NAACP). She was named Entertainer of the Year, and Best Supporting Actress in a Motion Picture for *Ghost*.

Goldberg now had a farm in Connecticut and an oceanfront house in Pacific Palisades, a section of Los Angeles where many people in show business live. Her Pacific Palisades home, which had stained-glass windows and was surrounded by landscaped gardens, was at the end of a private road. Inside, it was open and airy, with antique bookcases to hold Goldberg's many books. Goldberg reads a lot, and especially likes biographies. She collects rare books and has a special interest in first editions and children's books. She also collects art.

At this time Goldberg was involved in a relationship with cameraman Eddie Gold. She said it was going well because they were not with each other constantly. They were both so busy that most of the time when one of them was home, the other was working. Goldberg liked this because she needed time by herself, especially when she came home from work. For her, this was a time to enjoy some peace and quiet, a time to change from being Whoopi Goldberg to being Caryn Johnson.

Goldberg has often said that it is her young fans who know her best and understand who she is as a person and a performer. She has said, "They know I'm just as interested and as excited about the world and life as they are."[4] In her 1992 film *Sarafina!* she plays a teacher in South Africa who inspires children to learn more about their heritage, their world, and their lives.

Sarafina! had been a successful play, and Goldberg was drawn to the story. As with so many of her roles, Goldberg got this one by asking for it. After making the movie *Sarafina!*, she said that she was glad to have a part in it because she strongly believed in what the film said. People who did not like the movie's message might get angry, but that did not bother Goldberg. Her work had been making people angry since her days as a comedian in San Diego nightclubs. Now that she was acting in films, she wanted parts that angered people.[5]

People did get angry. But this time, they did more than just picket. Goldberg was the first American black actor to star in a film shot in South Africa. There had been a ten-year cultural boycott of South Africa to protest that country's system of segregation, called apartheid. The boycott was called off the year before Goldberg went to South Africa, but some groups wanted it to continue. One of these groups was AZAPO (Azanian People's Organization). Goldberg got AZAPO's approval to work in South Africa. By the time she arrived, however, AZAPO's members had changed their minds and were angry that she had come to South Africa. She was denounced in the newspapers and her passport was stolen. (It was later returned.)

After *Sarafina!* Goldberg made one of her biggest hits, *Sister Act* (1992), in which she plays Deloris, a lounge singer who witnesses a murder and goes to a convent to hide from gangsters. She later said, "I really wanted to do this because as I thought about the part, I knew it would be another dimension to add to the odd and bizarre career that I've made for myself. And in the process perhaps I would learn some things—which I did."[6]

In addition to being an enormous hit, *Sister Act* added a new dimension to Goldberg's career in another way: It was the first film in which she sang. Goldberg has never considered herself a professional singer. To prepare for her role in *Sister Act*, she practiced singing for an hour a day for one month.

Goldberg's 1993 film *Made in America* would help her prove something she had been saying for years. It would also lead to one of her most important relationships. The end of that relationship would be one of her biggest personal disappointments and most bitter public controversies.

Goldberg practiced singing one hour every day for a month to prepare for the filming of *Sister Act*.

9

THE HIGHEST-PAID ACTRESS IN HOLLYWOOD

ade in America was originally written for two white stars. For years, Goldberg had been saying that color should not matter when casting movies, but she was always told that it did matter. For years, she had been saying a black actor and a white actor could be paired romantically, but she was told this could not be done. When Goldberg let it be known that she was interested in a leading role in *Made in America*, she finally met a director who agreed with her. Richard Benjamin wanted Goldberg to be in his film because he believed she would make the movie better. He said that he could not think of any other American actress who had Goldberg's ability to play comedy and also show the serious side of a character. Many directors would have cast the film so it would have two black stars, but Benjamin was willing to cast Goldberg in one of the two leading roles and still have a white actor play the other leading role.

Goldberg's costar was Ted Danson, whom she had met in 1990 when they both appeared on *The Arsenio Hall Show*. At that time, Danson expressed great respect for Goldberg, and when they filmed *Made in America* his respect for her increased. As he got to know her better, he came to truly appreciate her honesty, her willingness to stand up for her opinions, and her determination to fight for what she believed in. While they were working on *Made in America*, Goldberg and Danson became romantically involved.

Before *Made in America* opened in the theaters, Goldberg had already moved on to her next project. In the summer of 1992, she announced plans to host a half-hour television talk show. Of course, she wanted her show to be different from all the other talk shows. Her show would not have a band, there would not be an announcer she could make funny remarks to, and there would not be an audience in the studio when the show was taped. There would be only one guest per show. Goldberg wanted to simply sit and have a real conversation with each person who appeared on her show. She wanted her guests to be able to talk about

Television host Whoopi Goldberg wanted *The Whoopi Goldberg Show* to be different from all the other talk shows.

anything they wanted and to say whatever was on their minds.

The Whoopi Goldberg Show premiered on September 14, 1992, with the actress Elizabeth Taylor as Goldberg's first guest. The reviews were not enthusiastic. One critic was disappointed in the questions Goldberg asked Taylor and said that Goldberg's skills as an interviewer needed to be improved.

In the following weeks, Goldberg's guests included many public figures and celebrities, such as Al Gore, Elton John, Lily Tomlin, Francis Ford Coppola, Bo Jackson, Robin Williams, Billy Crystal, Tim Robbins, Alexander Haig, Charlton Heston, Anthony Quinn, and John Travolta. But the show failed to gain popularity, and its ratings went steadily down.

Goldberg's response to the show's falling ratings was that she did not want her guests to feel they had to perform on her show. She did not want them to think they had to be as funny as she could be. She wanted to make her guests feel at ease, and she wanted them to just be themselves. Above all, Goldberg wanted the freedom to do the show as she pleased, not as others thought it should be done. She also wanted the artistic freedom to express herself in new ways, even if she was not perfect when she tried something new. She said, "I'm much happier to try all kinds of things. No, I'm not going to be great at everything, but that's O.K."[1]

In 1993, *The Whoopi Goldberg Show* was canceled, after two hundred episodes.

During her time as a talk show host, Goldberg tried something else that was new for her. She wrote a book for children, *Alice*, which was published in October 1992. A modern version of *Alice in Wonderland*, *Alice* is the story of a girl who thinks she would be really happy if she were rich. So she enters every contest and sweepstakes she can. Finally, she wins a sweepstakes and goes to New York City to claim her prize. There, she has many adventures that teach her what it really means to be happy.

When Goldberg wrote *Alice*, she wanted to create a fairy tale that had a young black girl as its central character. She wanted the girl to learn that having money is not as important as having a loving family and friends you can count on.

Still, the more rich and famous Goldberg became, the more difficult it was for her to find time to be with her own family and friends. When she did, it was hard to be alone with them, away from the prying media. People from the press were always asking questions. They always wanted interviews, always wanted to know what it was like to be Whoopi Goldberg. The press had helped make her famous. But she never hesitated to point out that the press also creates many problems for celebrities.

In 1993, she told an interviewer that reporters and

photographers had made it extremely difficult for her to be with her friends in public. Because of all the attention Goldberg received when she went out, she had become more comfortable spending time with her friends in the privacy of her own home. Here, they could say and do what they wanted without worrying that it would appear in newspapers and magazines or on television.

Only a few months later, Goldberg and the press became locked in their biggest battle yet. Goldberg belonged to a show business organization called the Friars Club. Sometimes the Friars Club holds a special dinner to pay tribute to one of its members. These dinners are called roasts, because people tell jokes and embarrassing stories about the guest of honor. On October 8, 1993, the Friars Club held a roast for Whoopi Goldberg.

Goldberg was still involved with Ted Danson. Together they wrote jokes about what it was like for a black woman and a white man to be in a relationship. When it was time for Danson to get up and "roast" Goldberg, he appeared with black makeup on his face (in "blackface"), pretending he was black. He then told the jokes that he and Goldberg had written together. But the jokes, and Danson's blackface, offended some of the guests at the roast. Danson was accused of being a racist, and the media played up the story for months.

Goldberg and Danson did not mean to cause such

a controversy, and she defended him. She told a writer for *Jet* magazine that there were a lot of people at the roast who were not familiar with what happens during these dinners. Goldberg reminded people that the purpose of a roast is to make fun of the person who is being honored. She pointed out that it is called a roast because the guest of honor is scorched by the jokes.[2]

A month after the roast, Goldberg and Danson ended their romantic relationship. The incident increased Goldberg's wariness of the press. In December 1993, an interviewer asked her whether the Friars Club roast had ended her relationship with Danson. She answered, "Questions like you've been asking me for the last five minutes, that's what ended my relationship with Ted."[3] Minutes before, Goldberg had been joking with the interviewer. When she said this, she was not joking at all.

The Friars Club roast was a major disappointment for Goldberg, but 1993 also brought one of her greatest triumphs. *Sister Act* had been so successful that the studio wanted to do a sequel. Of course, they wanted Goldberg to star, and she was paid $7 million for *Sister Act 2: Back in the Habit*. That year, Whoopi Goldberg became the highest-paid actress in Hollywood.

Yet she still remained philosophical about her success. She said that she was prepared for her success to end, and she often pointed out the times her projects had failed. In 1993, her career was at a high point, but she was well aware that a star's career has low points as well. She often reminded people that when she first started attracting attention as a performer, some people said she would not last in show business.

Goldberg had not only proved she would last but was even socializing with the president of the United States. In November, she was one of the hosts who greeted President Clinton at an annual party for the president at Ford's Theater in Washington, D.C. This was only one month after the Friars Club roast, and Goldberg knew that people in the audience were worried about what she might say. "I bet you're nervous, and I don't blame you, because you all know that I am truly politically incorrect," she joked after she walked onstage. Then she added, "A gala to honor the President, and they call me."[4]

In 1994, Whoopi Goldberg became both the first black person, and the first woman, to host the Oscars alone. As usual, the press was waiting to pounce. Before the telecast, there was speculation about whether she would say something outrageous. True to form, Goldberg refused to make any promises about what she might or might not say. In fact, from the way she was talking to interviewers, it seemed that she would indeed say something outrageous. In one interview she said that the Oscar ceremony was a perfect time for movie stars to tell the world that they think about real issues and are not self-centered people concerned only with how good their hair looks and how much money they make.[5]

But during the Oscars show, the usually outspoken Goldberg went to the opposite extreme. She was such a subdued host that many people were disappointed. Critics said she was too low-key. They complained that she was not controversial or even funny and that the show was boring. Perhaps people *wanted* her to be outrageous. Perhaps they were angry that she did not give them what they wanted. Once again, Goldberg was being attacked for not living up to people's expectations.

The year 1994 was a busy one for Goldberg. She appeared in six feature films, including two animated features in which she gave her voice to cartoon characters. In *The Lion King* she is the voice of Shenzi the hyena, and in *The Pagemaster* she is the voice of Fantasy.

Goldberg was busy off-camera, too. In September 1994, she married for the third time. She had met Lyle Trachtenberg, a union organizer for the movie and television technicians' union IATSE (International Alliance of Theatrical Stage Employees and Moving Picture Machine Operators), while she was making the film *Corrina, Corrina* (1994). On Labor Day weekend, she and Trachtenberg were married at her Pacific Palisades home in front of about 350 guests, including Arnold Schwarzenegger, Matthew Modine, Steven Spielberg, Natalie Cole, Jon Voight, Robin Williams,

Jay Leno, Richard Pryor, Maria Shriver, and Quincy Jones.

The guests could barely hear the ceremony because helicopters filled with tabloid reporters and photographers flew overhead, drowning out the couple as they said their vows. Goldberg told her new husband, "This is what you're going to get with me."[6]

Like her earlier marriages, this one was not to last. On October 26, 1995, a little more than a year after she and Trachtenberg were married, Goldberg quietly filed for divorce.

In 1995, Goldberg received a special honor. For decades, film stars have been asked to leave impressions of their hands and feet in the concrete outside Mann's Chinese Theatre in Los Angeles. Stars who are known for something special might also be asked to leave an impression of what they are known for. In 1995, Whoopi Goldberg left impressions of her hands, feet, and braids outside Mann's Chinese Theatre.

That December, Goldberg again went to Washington, D.C., where she joined Senator Ted Kennedy and Marian Wright Edelman (founder of the Children's Defense Fund) in a forum opposing a Republican plan to make big changes in welfare regulations. Goldberg told the forum, "The welfare system works. I know it works because I'm here. I'm proud of it. . . . The country was there for me, and the system worked for me."[7] She then challenged the people who wanted to change welfare regulations to sit down and talk with people who, like her, were actually once part of the welfare system.

In 1996, Goldberg was asked to host the Oscars again. She walked onstage dressed in an elegant black gown and wearing diamonds. When she stepped up to the microphone, Goldberg playfully asked the audience whether they had missed her when she had not hosted the Oscars the year before. Then she launched into a series of jokes about Hollywood, movies, and the people who make them. This time, she met people's expectations. Goldberg's monologue was a hit.

While making her 1996 film *Eddie*, Goldberg became romantically involved with her costar, Frank Langella. Two films later, she took on one of her most unusual roles yet—playing both a black woman and a white man—in *The Associate* (1996). For this film, to play the white man she wore so much makeup that sometimes even people who knew Goldberg did not recognize her. Once, when she was wearing her makeup and talking to her costar, Eli Wallach, he did not realize he was talking to Goldberg. When Hugh Wilson, who was Goldberg's director for *Burglar*, met her while she was made up as a man, he, too, did not recognize her.

As active as she was in films, Goldberg was still a stage performer and was still committed to helping the causes she believed in. In October 1996, she performed

In *The Associate*, Goldberg took on the challenge of playing a black woman who disguises herself as a white man.

at a benefit for Friends in Deed, which assists people with AIDS, cancer, and other serious illnesses. This show was directed by Mike Nichols, who had directed her on Broadway.

Goldberg performed some of her spooks, but she also pretended to be various famous women and invited the audience to ask these women questions. When people asked questions, Goldberg answered them as one of the famous women. At the end of the show, Goldberg portrayed a little girl who was dying. The girl wanted affection, but other children were afraid to touch her or even be near her. As the little girl, Goldberg went into the audience, and hugged and kissed a man who was seated near the stage. Then she asked him to pass the hug and kiss to the person next to him. Within a few minutes the hug and kiss traveled all the way across the front row of the theater.

10

NEW CHALLENGES

Whoopi Goldberg keeps taking on new challenges. In the film *Ghosts of Mississippi* (1996), for the first time in her career she portrayed a real person, playing Myrlie Evers, the widow of murdered civil rights activist Medgar Evers. Many critics were disappointed in both Goldberg and the film, and *Ghosts of Mississippi* was not as successful as people had expected it to be.

In 1997, Goldberg returned to Broadway. But this time she did not perform her own show or do her spooks. She starred in *A Funny Thing Happened on the Way to the Forum*, a musical comedy set in ancient Rome. She agreed to take over the part of the slave

Goldberg was cast as Myrlie Evers, widow of the murdered civil rights activist Medgar Evers, in *Ghosts of Mississippi*.

Pseudolus, who had been played by Nathan Lane. The show's producers kept this casting change secret.

On October 9, 1996, after the show's matinee performance, Lane came back onstage at the St. James Theater and told the audience that he was going to leave the show on February 11, but that he had exciting news to tell the people who were sitting in the theater. He then told them that he was being replaced by one of the world's funniest people—Whoopi Goldberg.

Goldberg walked out onto the stage dressed in a bright blue-and-white toga and leggings. As the audience cheered, she stood there, nodding and silently thanking everyone for their warm response.

Later, on the street outside the theater, Goldberg found herself surrounded by a crowd of fans who were eagerly anticipating her return to Broadway. As she got into a limousine, she mentioned to a reporter that she had not performed on a Broadway stage for twelve years. She was looking forward to it, but the prospect of returning to Broadway also scared her and made her nervous. She planned to do a lot of rehearsing during the coming months.[1]

In January 1997, Whoopi Goldberg, Candace Bergen, and Michael Douglas were cohosts at the 1997 Presidential Inaugural Gala—an entertainment industry tribute to Bill and Hillary Clinton. For the gala, Goldberg had to travel from her New York City rehearsals to Washington, D.C. When it looked as if Goldberg might arrive late, she was given an escort by state troopers through Delaware and Maryland. She arrived in Washington on time, and from the stage she told the President and Mrs. Clinton, and their daughter, Chelsea, "You're three of the coolest people I know."[2]

Goldberg is a frequent visitor to the White House. "I'm exactly the kind of person the Secret Service is paid to keep away from most presidents," she jokes.[3] She has known President Clinton for many years and counts herself among his friends. She has said that both the president and his wife are very funny people who like to laugh a lot. She has also said that she feels they are people who believe in change, and that she trusts them to do what they can to make this country better.[4]

Goldberg officially took over the role of Pseudolus in *A Funny Thing Happened on the Way to the Forum* on March 6, 1997. The part was originally written for a man, and the character is supposed to say the words written in the script. But Goldberg is known for improvising—and saying almost anything when she does. People wondered how she would do in a scripted show. Would she stick to the script, or would she say whatever popped into her head? Once again, Goldberg surprised people. When she went onstage as Pseudolus, she stuck to the script, stayed in character, and proved once more what she had been saying for years: Give her a good role, and she will deliver a good performance.

Goldberg was scheduled to leave *A Funny Thing Happened on the Way to the Forum* on June 29, 1997. President Clinton wanted to see her perform, but he could not get to the theater by that date. So the show was extended through July 13. The Democratic National Committee bought out the entire June 30 performance, and fifty-eight seats near the stage were removed so the president could easily get to his front-row seat before the show. The president's staff also took control of the wardrobe room and the stage manager's office, where secure phone lines were set up.

During the show, someone arrived late. Goldberg came out of character and said to him, "Any other night we would have waited for you, but we got the Prez. You get caught in traffic? You can talk to me. This is an interactive show." The man responded, "It's the President's fault." Goldberg answered, "I ain't touching that one."[5]

After the show, President Clinton and Vice President Al Gore went onstage. The president shook hands with the cast and hugged Goldberg affectionately.

In October 1997, Goldberg published a second book. Unlike *Alice*, this is not a children's story. Simply called *Book*, it is a collection of essays Goldberg has

Goldberg was both excited and nervous about her return to Broadway after twelve years. She took over a role originally written for a man in the show *A Funny Thing Happened on the Way to the Forum.*

written (she calls them riffs) in which she talks about her life and thoughts.

The following month, one of Goldberg's old riffs came to life when she played the queen in a new version of Rodgers and Hammerstein's *Cinderella*, which was televised on November 2, 1997. The show was cast without regard to color. Goldberg is a black queen with a white husband, and their son is played by a Filipino actor. Cinderella is played by the black singer Brandy, and her stepmother is played by actress Bernadette Peters, who is white. This production of Cinderella was exactly the kind of show Goldberg had dreamed of. It demonstrated that nontraditional casting works, even with a story that audiences know very well. And it proved something that Goldberg had been saying for years: If they want to do it, producers can choose an actor purely because of his or her talent, because art has no color.

In 1997, Goldberg sold an idea to CBS for a dramatic television series she called *Harlem*. She plans to star as the head of a large New York family that has both black and white people in it. She also agreed to coproduce and appear on a new version of the 1968 television game show *Hollywood Squares*. The show debuted on September 14, 1998, on CBS-TV.

Goldberg continues to try new things and to seek new creative directions. Yet in many ways she is the same person she was when she was growing up in New

York. "I'm a hippie," she says. "I was born a hippie and will be one till I die. . . . When I say hippie, I mean humanist. Environmentalist. Someone who wants world peace."[6]

Goldberg believes that people should try to make the world a better place, and that one person can do a lot. She remains an adamant supporter of women's rights and the right to an abortion, participating in protests and marches around the country. She has won numerous humanitarian awards for her charitable work, which includes raising money to help the homeless (to date, Comic Relief has raised more than $40 million), supporting AIDS research, making antidrug public service announcements, and giving benefit performances. She has raised money for victims of Hurricane Andrew in Florida, has given her own money to aid Rwandan refugees in Africa, and has served holiday dinners at homeless shelters in the United States. She is an active supporter of children's rights and works with Covenant House in Los Angeles, which helps troubled young people get off the streets, stay off the streets, and make better lives for themselves.

She continues to be outspoken, both onstage and off. "I don't set out to shock people," she has said. "It's just who I am, and I guess I'm somewhat shocking. I get in trouble speaking out, but I'd be in trouble with myself if I didn't."[7]

Goldberg is a dedicated artist who devotes a great

deal of time and energy to her craft. Show business is glamorous, but it is also hard work. Making films is a slow, repetitive process, and performing onstage takes a lot of concentration. Doing as many films and other projects as Goldberg has requires extraordinary commitment and effort that a star's fans are not always aware of.

In addition to winning one Oscar and being nominated for another, Goldberg has been nominated for six Emmy Awards. The Emmy Award is television's equivalent of the Oscar. One of Goldberg's Emmy nominations was for the episode "Hot Rod Brown" from the series *Tales from the Whoop*, which is broadcast on Nickelodeon, the cable channel for children and teens. Goldberg has won Nickelodeon's Kid's Choice Award for Favorite Movie Actress five times.

Some people have said that Goldberg is difficult to work with. She has admitted to losing her temper when things do not go right on a film or a show. But she said this is not because she is difficult. Rather, it is because she gets upset when people do not do their job, or do not do their job well. Poor work eats up energy that people could be using for good work. Goldberg does not think that being a star gives her the right to throw tantrums. She just wants any project she does to be as good as it can possibly be.

Goldberg continues to grapple with a problem many celebrities face: Every detail of her life is published, and the things that are said about her are not always accurate. This is especially upsetting when newspapers and magazines write about her family, her friends, or her romances. It takes a lot of hard work for anyone to maintain a good relationship. It is especially difficult for celebrities because the press constantly watches them and writes about everything they say and do.

Being famous has often put a strain on Goldberg's relationship with her daughter, Alexandrea, who is now married and had a second child, Jerzey, in 1996. While Goldberg was pursuing her career, Alexandrea was cared for by Goldberg's mother a good deal of the time. Goldberg has said, "It got rough. My kid felt overshadowed by Whoopi Goldberg. Every kid wants to do better than her parent. When you're Whoopi Goldberg's kid, that's hard to do."[8]

Their relationship began to improve when Goldberg made *Sister Act 2*. Alexandrea, who was then eighteen, had a small role in the film as one of the students. She accompanied Goldberg to the movie set every day, saw how much effort it takes to make a movie, and watched Goldberg fight, when necessary, to get the film done in a way that satisfied her. This gave Alexandrea a new appreciation for how hard her mother worked, and she began to think about their relationship differently.[9] Now that Alexandrea is an adult, with children of her own, Goldberg and her daughter have become closer.

Famous as she is, Goldberg still battles for good roles. Actor/director Bill Duke, who directed her in *Sister Act 2*, has said that Goldberg has gotten many roles by persuading people to give them to her.[10] Many times she was told she simply did not look like a typical Hollywood star. But she never let that stop her. She just kept fighting. She did not always win the fight, but she always gave it her best effort.

Goldberg still gets criticism about the films she does. People still ask why she does not appear in more films like *The Color Purple*. But many times that is not the kind of film she is offered. In this way Goldberg is still fighting one battle she has fought all her career. She is not always offered strong roles, but she is often criticized for the roles she decides to accept.

Goldberg continues to rebel against being called an African American. "I won't let anyone call me African American," she insists. "Because I'm not from Africa. Calling me an African American divides us further. . . . I don't have to excuse the fact that I am brown-skinned or black-skinned. I don't have to explain that. I was born here. I am as American as a hot dog. As baseball."[11]

Not all black people agree with her on the issue of black identity. Nevertheless, over the years Goldberg has won six Image Awards from the National Association for the Advancement of Colored People. And she has been an inspiration to many black women.

One black woman writer who has known her for years said that "she proves it is possible to move beyond limited definitions and stereotypes and create beauty and success—on our own terms."[12]

Stage and movie star, author, social and political activist, philanthropist, mother and grandmother, Goldberg's life has been one of extremes. She has gone from poverty, drugs, and welfare to wealth, stardom, and international fame. She has offended people and won their admiration. In an industry where image and pretension are common, she has stubbornly remained her own person, breaking the rules but succeeding anyway. She is a star who does not behave like a star, a black person who will not allow herself to be labeled as one.

In fact, Goldberg does not want to be labeled as any one thing. "Labels don't give you any room to grow at all," she believes.[13] When it comes to her career and her life, she feels that anything is possible. The important thing is for people to keep their choices open and, above all, to learn from whatever they decide to do.

Whoopi Goldberg is still learning. Reflecting on all the different things she has done, she has said, "You try something and get hit in the face with a pie, and so you realize that's not the way to do it. You go in another direction and get hit again. Finally, you find a road where you just get a fleck of pie, a little crumb. That's what I'm working toward."[14]

Perhaps the best way to sum up Whoopi Goldberg is with the words inscribed on the honorary degree she received in 1985 from the University of Charleston in West Virginia: "To experience Whoopi Goldberg is to expand your mind, awaken your conscience and view the world through new eyes."[15]

Chronology

1955—Born Caryn Johnson, in New York City, on November 13.

1964—Starts performing in the children's theater group at the Hudson Guild.

1982—First performs *The Spook Show*, at the Hawkeye Theater in Berkeley, California.

1983—*Moms* opens at the Hawkeye Theater in Berkeley.

1984—Wins a Bay Area Critics' Award for *Moms*; performs *The Spook Show* at the Dance Theater Workshop in New York City; *Whoopi Goldberg* opens at the Lyceum Theater on Broadway.

1985—Is nominated for an Academy Award for Best Actress for *The Color Purple* but does not win; wins a Grammy Award for Best Comedy Recording for *Whoopi Goldberg: Original Broadway Show*; wins her first NAACP Image Award (by 1992, she will have won six Image Awards); wins a Golden Globe Award for Best Performance by an Actress for *The Color Purple;* receives an honorary degree from the University of Charleston in West Virginia.

1986—Helps organize Comic Relief, an organization to raise money for the homeless; is nominated for her first Emmy Award (by 1994, she will have been nominated for six Emmys).

1988—Joins the cast of *Star Trek: The Next Generation*, in the role of Guinan, the psychic bartender.

1990—Stars in her own television series, *Bagdad Cafe*; wins a Golden Globe Award for Best Supporting Actress for *Ghost*.

1991—Wins the Academy Award for Best Supporting Actress for *Ghost*.

1992—*The Whoopi Goldberg Show* premieres with Goldberg as a television talk show host; children's book *Alice* is published.

1993—Is paid $7 million for *Sister Act 2*, becoming the highest-paid actress in Hollywood.

1994—Becomes the first black person, and the first woman, to host the Oscars alone.

1995—Impressions of Goldberg's hands, feet, and braids are made in concrete outside Mann's Chinese Theatre in Los Angeles.

1996—Hosts the Oscars for the second time.

1997—Returns to Broadway, taking over the role of Pseudolus in *A Funny Thing Happened on the Way to the Forum*; autobiographical *Book* is published; wins a special People's Choice Award honoring her career in film, television, and stage. Since 1993, she has won six People's Choice Awards.

1998—Hosts the television game show *Hollywood Squares*.

FILMOGRAPHY

Selected Films

The Color Purple, 1985
  (Oscar nomination, Best Actress)
Jumpin' Jack Flash, 1986
Burglar, 1987
Fatal Beauty, 1987
The Telephone, 1988
Clara's Heart, 1988
Kiss Shot, 1989
Beverly Hills Brats, 1989
The Long Walk Home, 1990
Ghost, 1990
  (Oscar, Best Supporting Actress)
Homer and Eddie, 1990
Soapdish, 1991
House Party 2, 1991
The Player, 1992
Sarafina!, 1992
Sister Act, 1992
Wisecracks, 1992
Made in America, 1993
Sister Act 2: Back in the Habit, 1993
The Lion King, 1994
The Little Rascals, 1994

Corrina, Corrina, 1994

Star Trek Generations, 1994

The Pagemaster, 1994

Boys on the Side, 1995

Moonlight and Valentino, 1995

The Celluloid Closet, 1996
   (Narrator)

Eddie, 1996

Theodore Rex, 1996

Bogus, 1996

The Associate, 1996

Ghosts of Mississippi, 1996

In the Gloaming, 1997

Rodgers and Hammerstein's *Cinderella,* 1997

In & Out, 1997

An Alan Smithee Film . . . Burn Hollywood Burn, 1998

How Stella Got Her Groove Back, 1998

Selected Television Roles
Star Trek: The Next Generation (1988–1994)

Bagdad Cafe (1990–1991)

Captain Planet and the Planeteers (1990–1995)

The Whoopi Goldberg Show (1992–1993)

Hollywood Squares (1998–   )

CHAPTER NOTES

Chapter 1. A Big Night at the Oscars

1. Janet Maslin, "Ghost," *The New York Times*, July 13, 1990, p. C8.

2. Sheila Benson, "An Afterlife Love Story," *Los Angeles Times*, July 13, 1990, p. F13.

3. Desson Howe, "Ghost," *Washington Post*, July 13, 1990, p. 48.

4. Mason Wiley and Damien Bona, *Inside Oscar: The Unofficial History of the Academy Awards* (New York: Ballentine Books, 1996), p. 801.

5. Ibid., p. 803.

6. Nina J. Easton, "'Dances With Wolves', Irons, Bates Win Oscars," *Los Angeles Times*, March 26, 1991, p. A21.

7. Elaine Dutka and David J. Fox, "Behind-the-Scenes Vignettes at the Academy Awards," *Los Angeles Times*, March 26, 1991, p. F3.

8. Ibid.

9. Ibid.

Chapter 2. Growing Up in New York

1. Paul Chutkow, "Remaking Whoopi," *Vogue*, January 1991, p. 181.

2. Whoopi Goldberg, *Book* (New York: Rob Weisbach Books, William Morrow and Company, 1997), p. 37.

3. Jamie Diamond, "Whoopi Goldberg," *Cosmopolitan*, November 1992, p. 210.

4. Goldberg, p. 40.

5. Diamond, p. 210.

6. Edward Guthmann, "A Comic's Uncanny Replay of Moms Mabley," *San Francisco Chronicle*, May 27, 1984, p. 23.

7. David Rensin, "Playboy Interview: Whoopi Goldberg," *Playboy*, June 1987, p. 154.

8. Ibid.

9. Ibid., p. 155.

10. Cathleen McGuigan, "The Whoopi Comedy Show," *Newsweek*, March 5, 1984, p. 63.

Chapter 3. A New Life in California

1. Guy Trebay, "The Whoopi Goldberg Variations," *Village Voice*, October 30, 1984, p. 54.

2. David Rensin, "Playboy Interview: Whoopi Goldberg," *Playboy*, June 1987, p. 52.

3. Pamela Noel, "Who Is Whoopi Goldberg and What Is She Doing on Broadway???" *Ebony*, March 1985, p. 30.

4. "Goldberg, Whoopi," *Current Biography Yearbook 1985* (New York: H. W. Wilson Company, 1985), p. 145.

5. Rensin, pp. 156–157.

6. "Whoopi Goldberg," *People*, December 23–30, 1985, p. 102.

Chapter 4. Back to New York

1. Janet Coleman, "Making Whoopi," *Vanity Fair*, July 1984, p. 108.

2. "Whoopi Goldberg," *Interview*, December 1984, p. 76.

3. Mel Gussow, "Stage: Whoopi Goldberg Does 'The Spook Show,'" *The New York Times*, February 3, 1984, p. C3.

4. *People*, August 13, 1984, p. 106.

5. Edward Guthmann, "A Comic's Uncanny Replay of Moms Mabley," *San Francisco Chronicle*, May 27, 1984, p. 23.

Chapter 5. Back to Broadway

1. "Whoopi Goldberg," *Interview*, December 1984, p. 75.

2. Clive Barnes, "This Season's Cult Star in the Makin': Whoopi," *New York Post*, October 25, 1984.

3. Guy Trebay, "The Whoopi Goldberg Variations," *Village Voice*, October 30, 1984, p. 54.

4. Audrey Edwards, "Whoopi!" *Essence*, March 1985, p. 85.

5. Enid Nemy, "Whoopi's Ready, But Is Broadway?" *The New York Times*, October 21, 1984, sec. 2, p. 4.

6. "Magazine Names 'Best' Californians," *San Francisco Chronicle*, November 6, 1984, p. 2.

7. Stephen M. Silverman, "Whoopi's on a Roll, and Does She Love It," *New York Post*, November 7, 1984, p. 29.

8. David Rensin, "Playboy Interview: Whoopi Goldberg," *Playboy*, June 1987, p. 56.

Chapter 6. Whoopi Goldberg: Film Star

1. Diana Maychick, "'Color Purple' Is Making Whoopi as Good as Gold," *New York Post,* January 7, 1986, p. 23.
2. Jill Kearney, "Color Her Anything," *American Film,* December 1985, p. 26.
3. Steve Erickson, "Whoopi Goldberg," *Rolling Stone,* May 8, 1986, p. 92.
4. Bob Thomas, "Whoopi: Humor 'Just a Fluke,'" *New York Post,* October 29, 1986.
5. Pat H. Broeske, "Whoopi Wises Up," *Los Angeles Times,* April 22, 1990, p. 88.
6. "Whoopi Goldberg," *People,* December 23–30, 1985, p. 100.

Chapter 7. A Career Fades

1. Pamela Noel, "Who Is Whoopi Goldberg and What Is She Doing on Broadway???" *Ebony,* March 1985, p. 34.
2. "Whoopi Goldberg Doesn't Put Any Limits on Herself," *San Francisco Chronicle,* January 3, 1986, p. 61.
3. Steve Erickson, "Whoopi Goldberg," *Rolling Stone,* May 8, 1986, pp. 40, 92.
4. Lindsy Van Gelder, "I'm Whoopi and You're Not," *New York Daily News Magazine,* December 22, 1985, p. 13.
5. Vincent Canby, "Whoopi Goldberg in 'Jumpin' Jack Flash,'" *The New York Times,* October 10, 1986, p. C7.
6. Vincent Canby, "Whoopi Goldberg in 'Burglar,'" *The New York Times,* March 20, 1987, p. C10.
7. "Whoopi Goldberg Target of Pickets," *Los Angeles Times,* March 22, 1987, sec. 2, p. 6.
8. Stephen M. Silverman, "Whoopi's Cushion," *New York Post,* October 27, 1987, p. 33.
9. "Whoopi Goldberg and Sam Elliott Star in 'Fatal Beauty,' A Humor-Laced Drama," *Jet,* November 16, 1987, p. 58.
10. "Whoopi Goldberg Says Her Teen Daughter Is Pregnant," *Jet,* November 20, 1989, p. 22.
11. Deborah Norville, "Girl Talk With Whoopi Goldberg," *McCall's,* June 1993, p. 162.
12. Jeremy Gerard, "'Comic Relief': Being Funny for a Serious Cause," *The New York Times,* May 11, 1990, p. C34.

Chapter 8. Comeback

1. David Sheff, "Playboy Interview: Whoopi Goldberg," *Playboy,* January 1997, p. 55.

2. Edward Guthmann, "Whoopi Hits Gold Again," *San Francisco Chronicle*, November 18, 1990, p. 22.

3. Ibid., p. 21.

4. Paul Chutkow, "Remaking Whoopi," *Vogue,* January 1991, p. 219.

5. "Whoopi Goldberg Stars as a Heroic Teacher to Leleti Khumalo in 'Sarafina' Film," *Jet,* September 28, 1992, p. 55.

6. "Whoopi Goldberg Becomes a Nun to Escape the Mob in 'Sister Act,'" *Jet,* June 1, 1992, p. 36.

Chapter 9. The Highest-Paid Actress in Hollywood

1. Isabel Wilkerson, "Staying Cool at Whoopi's Talk Show," *The New York Times*, November 29, 1992, p. C27.

2. "Whoopi Goldberg Defends Ted Danson's Blackface Act at Friars Club Roast," *Jet,* October 25, 1993, p. 13.

3. Stephen Schaefer, "The $7M Woman," *New York Post,* December 7, 1993, p. 33.

4. Nadine Brozan, "Whoopi Goldberg Goes to Washington to Help Honor the President," *The New York Times*, November 1, 1993, p. B10.

5. Dennis McDougal, "Whoopi Takes On Hollywood," *TV Guide*, March 19, 1994, p. 36.

6. "Lovable Lyle," *People,* October 17, 1994, p. 52.

7. "Goldberg, Kennedy Oppose Republicans' Welfare Proposal," *Jet,* December 25, 1995–January 1, 1996, p. 33.

Chapter 10. New Challenges

1. Ward Morehouse III, "Whoopi-do! She's Headin' to 'Forum,'" *New York Post,* October 10, 1996, p. 50.

2. Marc Sandalow, "D.C. Party in Full Swing, Tens of Thousands Brave the Bitter Cold," *San Francisco Chronicle*, January 20, 1997, p. A1.

3. David Sheff, "Playboy Interview: Whoopi Goldberg," *Playboy,* January 1997, p. 52.

4. Ibid.

5. Bruce Weber, "Laughing All the Way to a Fund-Raiser," *The New York Times*, July 1, 1997, p. B2.

4 sdsdsdsdsdd dsdsdddsdsddsdsd

6. David Rensin, "Playboy Interview: Whoopi Goldberg," *Playboy,* June 1987, p. 154.

7. Nancy Mills, "Habit Forming," *New York Daily News,* September 6, 1992, p. 15.

8. Bebe Moore Campbell, "Whoopi Talks B(l)ack," *Essence,* January 1997, p. 102.

9. Ibid.

10. Ibid.

11. Sheff, p. 180.

12. Audrey Edwards, "An Appreciation: Why Whoopi?" *Essence,* January 1997, p. 58.

13. Lindsy Van Gelder, "I'm Whoopi and You're Not," *New York Daily News Magazine,* December 22, 1985, p. 13.

14. Stephen Farber, "Making It Again!" *Cosmopolitan,* March 1991, p. 187.

15. "Whoopi Goldberg," *People,* December 23–30, 1985, p. 100.

FURTHER READING

Adams, Mary Agnes. *From Street to Stardom: Whoopi Goldberg*. New York: Dillon Press, 1993.

Blue, Rose, and Corinne J. Naden. *Whoopi Goldberg: Entertainer*. New York: Chelsea House Publishers, 1995.

Goldberg, Whoopi. *Alice*. New York: Bantam Books, 1992.

Katz, Sandor. *Whoopi Goldberg*. New York: Chelsea House Publishers, 1997.

Internet Addresses

The ACME Whoopi Page
<http://www.maikon.net/spreng/whoopi/index.html>

Celeb Site Profile
<http://www.celebsite.com/people/WhoopiGoldberg/index.html>

The Network for Entertainment Fans
<http://www.fansites.com/whoopi_goldberg.html>

Whoopi Page
<http://www.tu-berlin.de/~gruhlke/forum/whoopi/>

INDEX